MW01293953

31 Days With the Holy Spirit

A Daily Meditations and Prayers to Learn More of the Holy Spirit, Connect More With Him, and Manifest His Presence and Gifts

Daniel C. Okpara

Copyright © January 2019 by Daniel C. Okpara.
All Rights Reserved. Kindly note that the contents of this book should not be reproduced in any way or by any means without obtaining written consent from the author or his representative. However, brief excerpts for church or Christian references can be used without written permission.

Published By:

Better Life Media.

BETTER LIFE WORLD OUTREACH CENTER.

Website: www.BetterLifeWorld.org

Email: info@betterlifeworld.org

FOLLOW US ON FACEBOOK

1. Like our Page on Facebook for updates

2. Join Our Facebook Prayer Group, submit prayer requests and follow powerful daily prayers for total victory and breakthrough

This title and others are available for quantity discounts for sale promotions, gifts, and evangelism. Visit our website or email us to get started.

Any scripture quotation used in this book is taken from the New King James Version, except where stated. Used by permission.

Table of Contents

RECEIVE DAILY AND WEEKLY PRAYERS

Powerful Prayers Sent to Your Inbox Every Monday

Enter your email address to receive notifications of new posts, prayers and prophetic declarations sent to you by email.

Email Address

Sign Me Up

*Go to: **www.BreakThroughPrayers.org** to subscribe to receive FREE WEEKLY PRAYER POINTS, and prophetic declarations sent to you by email.*

FREE BOOKS ...

Download These 4 Powerful Books Today for FREE... Take Your Relationship With God to a New Level.

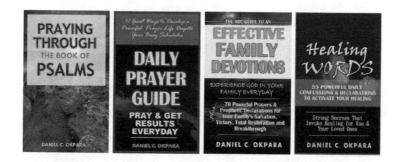

www.betterlifeworld.org/grow

Prologue

The theme of our October 2019 convention was Higher Heights. God spoke to my heart that it was time to forget what lies behind and reach forward to what lies ahead. There are depths to discover and heights to attain. But this must begin with a vigorous re-investment of self in the Word. We can never find God outside His Word. We can never attain any height or receive any blessing that we do not first encounter in the Word.

So I wrote this book and the entire *Higher Heights* series with one burden in my heart: *To help you encounter the depths of God that will transform your life and cause your destiny to begin to speak loud and clear.*

In these series, I teach on specific subjects over a 31-day period and lead us to pray the connecting lessons and scriptures into our lives. You will not only learn these subjects better, you will encounter a special revelation of God that will redefine your purpose and re-empower you to encounter your miracle and breakthrough.

I speak to hundreds of people every week, both from the counseling table and from the pulpit. I see the hurts and pains in the faces of people every time. I see the efforts and struggles they are making to give their lives a meaning. And I see the obvious failures, confusions, and questions.

As usual, my goal in all my meetings has always been to reveal Him who can help us through His Word. An encounter with Him is the key to all-round transformation. So get ready for a journey of deeper spiritual awareness, revelation and divine encounter.

While reading and praying with this book, expect to have a deeper understanding of the subject being discussed, expect to hear the voice of God, and expect to experience unprecedented breakthrough - spiritually and physically.

How to Use This Book

How do you read this book and others in the series so as to get the best value from them?

1. Start by reading this devotional every night before you go to bed for the next 31 days.

2. When you complete the first 31-day circle, come back and read it again, this time, read it early in the morning before step out of your bed.

3. You may read it in addition to your other devotionals.

4. Be consistent and try not to skip any day. If you do, come back and start from where you stopped.

5. Meditate on the Bible verses and short exhortations and ask the Lord for better understanding and revelation. Don't just rush them. Think on the scriptures and the lessons.

6. Pray the prayers and make the declarations that follow each day.

7. Mark points and statements that strike your spirit as you read and study.

8. Ask the Lord for help to make any corrections in your life, or carry out any instruction that you encounter each day. Remember, reading the word is good, but doing the word is better; because it is the doing that guarantees the results.

9. When you are done, come back again and again and repeat the process until the lessons and instructions begins to speak in your life.

Introduction

This is something that will change your life forever.

When God recommends someone to you, then you need to pay attention.

> And I will ask the Father, and he will give you another advocate to help you and be with you forever – John 14:16 - NIV

The Holy Spirit is not just your conscience; He is not a wind, and He is not a force that pushes people down. He is the One whose help you'll ever need if you must amount to anything in your Christian life.

Without Him, you'll struggle every day of your life.

As a Christian, you may have heard so much about the Holy Spirit. You may even speak so greatly of Him. And of course, read of Him in almost every Christian literature.

However, in your daily life, do you experience Him?

In this 31 days with the Holy Spirit devotional, let us attentively have a chat with the Holy Spirit is. Let us commune with Him, and experience His work in our lives in a different new way.

Note that these teachings are culled from my other publications. But the words are fresh as ever. As you read these daily insights and pray the attendant prayers, come to God with an open heart. Expect a special encounter with the Holy Spirit that will change your life forever.

Other Books in This Series

=> 31Days in the School of Faith.

=> 31 Days in the Parables.

=> 31 Days with the Heroes of Faith.

=> 31 Days With Jesus.

It's time to experience a new encounter with God that will change your life forever.

Day 1: Who is the Holy Spirit?

"For there are three that bear witness in heaven: the Father, the Word, and the Holy Spirit; and these three are one." - 1 John 5:7

Before we go deep into the subject of the Holy Spirit, let us first of all correct an erroneous assumption that some people hold about the Holy Spirit. The other day, a brother was earnestly arguing with others about the Holy Spirit. He was trying to convince his listeners that the Holy Spirit is just air or human conscience and nothing more. His listeners, though could not talk from scriptures, thought otherwise. Hence the heated argument. I interrupted the discussion and explained to them the truth about the Holy Spirit and the tension subsided.

The Holy Spirit is not just air, thought, fire, force, or water. Though He can impress in your conscience, He is not just your conscience. Though He can manifest as a wind, He is not wind. He is not water, and He is not handkerchief or oil.

The Holy Spirit is a Person, a Being, an entity who speaks, hears, communicates, and responds. He is the third Person in Godhead. He was there during Creation.

> In the beginning, God created the heavens and the earth. The earth was without form and void, and darkness was on the face of the deep. And the Spirit of God was hovering over the face of the waters. – Genesis 1:1-2

When it was time to create man, God spoke to His members in the Godhead:

> Then God said, "Let Us make man in Our image, according to Our likeness; let them have dominion over the fish of the sea, over the birds of the air, and over the cattle, over all the earth and over every creeping thing that creeps on the earth." - Genesis 1:26

God wasn't speaking to air, or to oil. He was speaking to "US" in the Godhead.

In today's memory verse, we read that "... there are three that bear witness in heaven: the Father, the Word, and the Holy Spirit; and these three are one."

This doesn't mean that there are three Gods. No. It means that we have three separate personalities in one God. However, even though they are separate, they are always in agreement.

As we get started in learning about the Holy Spirit, let us settle with the truth that the Holy Spirit is a person. Only a person hears, guides, teaches, instructs, reveals things, and comforts.

Declaration

Dear Heavenly Father,

I begin a quest today to know more about the Holy Spirit. I confess that I am limited as a human. So I ask for Your revelation and guidance as I learn about the Holy Spirit this month.

Holy Spirit, please teach me about Yourself. I realize that there are so many opinions and theological views when it comes to You. But I am relaxed today knowing that I will come to the knowledge of the truth as I seek to know You more. I will surely encounter Your person this month, and my life will never remain the same, in Jesus name.

Amen.

Day 2: The Holy Spirit and the Godhead

Then God said, "Let Us make man in Our image, according to Our likeness; let them have dominion over the fish of the sea, over the birds of the air, and over the cattle, over all the earth and over every creeping thing that creeps on the earth." - Genesis 1:26

As we noted yesterday, God wasn't speaking to air, or to angels here. He was speaking to the members of the Godhead, the Father, the Son, and the Holy Spirit.

We use the word, **Godhead**, many times to mean the same thing as "Trinity." While the term "trinity" is not found in the Scriptures per se, the idea is there. It is the doctrine that states that God exists as the Father, the Son, and the Holy Spirit. They are three separate Divine Persons who co-exist equally as One. They are not three Gods. There is only One God. But He is manifest as the Father, the Son, and the Holy Spirit.

The *Trinity* doctrine is something usually best discussed in Bible Schools and not in daily devotionals. However, since we are dedicating this month to learn about the Holy Spirit, who is a member of the Godhead, it is appropriate to let the Scripture speak to us on every aspect that will aid our understanding of who the Holy Spirit is.

The Holy Spirit in the Godhead

1. Matthew 28:18-19 - ₁₉Go therefore and make disciples of all the nations, baptizing them in the name of the Father and of the Son and of the Holy Spirit, ₂₀teaching them to observe all things that I have commanded you; and lo, I am with you always, even to the end of the age." Amen.

This is Jesus instructing His disciples to carry on His work of making disciples in every nation. He instructs them to baptize everyone who believes in the name of the Father, the Son, and the Holy Spirit.

Here, the Holy Spirit is recognized as a member of the Godhead whose place is essential in our teaching and making disciples of all nations. I believe that we can't become (or make effective) disciples without the work of   the   Holy   Spirit.

---

2. Matthew 3:16-17 – When He had been baptized, Jesus came up immediately from the water; and behold, the heavens were opened to Him, and He saw the Spirit of God descending like a dove and alighting upon Him. And suddenly a voice came from heaven, saying, "This is My beloved Son, in whom I am well pleased."

Again, the three persons of the Godhead are revealed here. The Son is baptized, the Holy Spirit comes as a Dove, and the Father speaks from heaven. This is a clear message that the work that Christ had come to do on earth is a work that the three are involved in. We see here also that they are separate persons but united in mission and purpose.

---

3. 2 Corinthians 13:14 - The grace of the Lord Jesus Christ, and the love of God, and the communion of the Holy Spirit be with you all. Amen.

The Apostle Paul, in this verse, also recognizes the trinity. He says:

- The grace of the Lord Jesus Christ

- The Love of God, and

- The communion (fellowship) of the Holy Spirit

He prayed that all of these three would be with us.

---

4. **John 14:16-17, 26** - And I will pray the Father, and he shall give you another Comforter, that he may abide with you forever; ₁₇ Even the Spirit of truth; whom the world cannot receive, because it seeth him not, neither knoweth him: but ye know him; for he dwelleth with you, and shall be in you.

₂₆ But the Comforter, which is the Holy Ghost, whom the Father will send in my name, he shall teach you all things, and bring all things to your remembrance, whatsoever I have said unto you.

5. John 15:26 - But when the Comforter is come, whom I will send unto you from the Father, even the Spirit of truth, which proceeds from the Father, he shall testify of me.

In these scriptures, Jesus, the Son, tells us to recognize the Holy Spirit. He is from the Father and is on earth now teaching us and testifying about the Son.

The implication of the above scriptures is that:

- The Holy Spirit is a member of the Godhead.

- He is involved in the work of creation and restoration of all things back to God

- He is the current member of the Godhead on earth testifying about Christ.

Consequently, understanding and appreciating the ministry of the Holy Spirit in our lives is essential for us to become effective Christians.

Declaration

Dear Holy Spirit,

I surrender to You from this day forward and receive Your ministry in my life. Teach me, and make manifest unto me God's glory and power so that I may be built up and established in You, in Jesus name.

Today, I declare that the grace of the Lord Jesus Christ, the Love of God, and the communion of the Holy Spirit will abide with me forever and ever, in Jesus name.

Amen.

Day 3: The Importance of the Holy Spirit

"If you then, being evil, know how to give good gifts to your children, how much more will your heavenly Father give the Holy Spirit to those who ask Him!" - Luke 11:13

If you read this Scripture in the Gospel of Matthew without looking it up here and other places, you'd think Jesus was talking about giving us every earthly thing that we'd ever ask. You'd think He meant that if we ask for rice and beans, houses and clothes, positions and money, God will hurriedly release those things for us since He's not a bad Father.

However, Luke adds a dimension in Jesus' sermon that helps us process His Truth embedded there. While God is not against us acquiring earthly things, Jesus is saying that the Holy Spirit is the key to receiving everything we'll ever need in life. His words here can be put this way:

- "I know you need bread and fish (daily foods)

- "I know you need houses, jobs, clothes, cars, and money...

- "But focus on receiving the Holy Spirit. He is the Gift that manifests every other gift. He is the Promise that manifests every other promise of God for us."

You now see that when Jesus said to seek the Kingdom of God first and every other thing will be added unto us, He is saying, *"Seek the Holy Spirit and His ministry in your life. Then every other thing you'll ever need will be added to you."*

Why?

Because "...His divine power has given to us all things that pertain to life and godliness, through the knowledge of Him who called us by glory and virtue" (2 Peter 1:3).

God has released to us everything that we will ever need to live a fulfilled life here on earth. He has given us every grace, connection, and wisdom to enable us live a Godly life. But the Holy Spirit is the key to accessing all of them.

Therefore, seek the Holy Spirit, and through Him, you will be able to access every one of the gifts, promises, and blessings that God has given to us. The Holy Spirit is the embodiment of all the promises of God in Scriptures.

Declaration

Precious Father, I thank You for revealing Your Word to me today. I now see that the Holy Spirit is the completeness of all Your promises, gifts, and blessings to us. Forgive me, Lord, for thinking otherwise.

Holy Spirit, henceforth, I seek to know You and receive Your ministry in my life. Thank You for being here to help me in every way I'll need help, in Jesus name.

Amen.

Day 4: Like a Dove

₁₆When He had been baptized, Jesus came up immediately from the water; and behold, the heavens were opened to Him, and He saw the Spirit of God descending like a dove and alighting upon Him. ₁₇And suddenly a voice came from heaven, saying, "This is My beloved Son, in whom I am well pleased." -
Matthew 3:16-17

In this scripture, the Holy Spirit manifested using a form of Dove. He is not a dove, so we don't get to look for doves and say, we've got Him. However, there are essential qualities of the dove that can teach us some things about the Holy Spirit.

1. **The dove was used by the poor for sacrifice.** Even if anyone could not afford other animals for offering, they could afford the dove. So God was

teaching us that the Holy Spirit is a gift for us all. We do not buy Him with money.

2. The dove was a bird of purity. It is never found in contaminated places. Same way, the Holy Spirit is "*Holy,*" that is, clean, pure, and wholesome. He dwells in vessels that are clean and free from contamination.

3. The dove is an innocent, harmless creature. It never hurts the least bird with which it comes into contact. The Holy Spirit is compared to a dove because He is kind, gentle, and harmless. His influence empowers us to be gentle and kind.

4. The dove has very keen eyesight. It sees from very far distances and protects itself from harm. The Holy Spirit sees ahead and "searches all things." He protects us from evil by informing us of things to come in advance.

5. The dove is a symbol of peace. The dove brought the olive shoot back in her mouth, indicating to Noah that the waters had waned and that the flood would soon be gone. The Holy Spirit is our only access to peace in this peace-less and hurting world. He quiets our mind and frees us from anxiety and worry, assuring us of our salvation and access to God. He keeps our hearts at peace with God, with ourselves and with others.

6. Doves are also given to mourning (Isaiah 38:14). "In the same way, the Spirit helps us in our weakness. We do not know what we ought to pray for, but the Spirit himself intercedes for us through wordless groans" (Rom. 8:26). The Holy Spirit takes up our infirmities, empowers our intercession, and heals us.

Declaration

Dear Holy Spirit,

I ask You to do Your work in my life and glorify Jesus Christ.

I declare that I have peace that passes all understanding.

I am protected from every form of harm, and safe in You Lord, in Jesus name.

Amen.

Day 5: Like Water

₃₇On the last day, that great day of the feast, Jesus stood and cried out, saying, "If anyone thirsts, let him come to Me and drink. ₃₈He who believes in Me, as the Scripture has said, out of his heart will flow rivers of living water." ₃₉But this He spoke concerning the Spirit, whom those believing in Him would receive; for the Holy Spirit was not yet given, because Jesus was not yet glorified. - John 7:37-39

The Holy Spirit is symbolized as water in Scriptures. In addition to the key verse for today, here are a few more scriptures to consider:

Isaiah 44:3 - For I will pour water on him who is thirsty and floods on the dry ground; I will pour My Spirit on your descendants, and My blessing on your offspring.

John 4:13-14 - ₁₃ Jesus answered and said to her, "Whoever drinks of this water will thirst again, ₁₄ but whoever drinks of the water that I shall give him will never thirst. But the water that I shall give him will become in him a fountain of water springing up into everlasting life."

1 Corinthians 12:13 - For by one Spirit we were all baptized into one body, whether Jews or Greeks, whether slaves or free, and we were all made to drink of one Spirit.

We know that water has many useful purposes. But from these references we see that the water the Bible refers to include the following three of these figures:

- Water that quenches a person's spiritual thirst,

- Water that facilitates a person's spiritual re-birth, and

- Water that cleanses from spiritual filthiness.

As we cannot live for long without water, so can we not survive without the Holy Spirit. He is the only One who can satisfy our spiritual thirst, answer our many questions about life, and inspire hope in us.

Declaration

I declare today that I cannot do without You Holy Spirit. You are all I ever need in life. As You know, I have many unanswered questions about myself, my life, and my future. Today, Holy Spirit, I am trusting You for answers that will pacify my thirst, in Jesus name,

Amen.

Day 6: Like a Mighty Rushing Wind

₂When the Day of Pentecost had fully come, they were all with one accord in one place. ₂ And suddenly there came a sound from heaven, as of a rushing mighty wind, and it filled the whole house where they were sitting. - Acts 2:1-2

On the day of Pentecost, the Holy Spirit came with a sound of a mighty rushing wind.

Consider how vital wind has been to the development of life. If there are no winds, exploration will not happen. The ships of the past had no mechanical energy to drive them, yet they glided across waters with easiness as their sails caught the winds. Men set sail and conquered the world by the force of the wind.

The wind is essential for advancement to be made. In fact, without wind blowing, there will be no movement. Without wind, we will be hundreds of years behind where we are today.

The Wind of the Spirit

Wind cannot be seen, but its effects can be heard and felt - just like the Holy Spirit. We cannot see Him, but we can see and feel the impact of His power and presence.

Just as the wind moves ships, enables engines, energizes windmills, and diffuses pollution from the earth, when the Holy Spirit came on the Day of Pentecost, His power transformed 120 disciples into a mighty force for God.

The wind is a symbol of force and power. That day the apostles were filled with power, and it became the most significant move of the time.

The wind symbol and manifestation of the Holy Spirit signify power that turns ordinary things into extraordinary tools. Remember that before this manifestation, the disciples were afraid of sharing the Gospel which they were eyewitnesses. But after that day, they were filled with extra-ordinary audaciousness; they went from place to place speaking boldly about Jesus Christ, His death, resurrection, and the kingdom of God.

Today, pray for the wind of the Holy Spirit to blow upon your life, your ministry, and your career. When the wind of the Holy Spirit blows upon anybody, a church, a business, or an idea, it blows life back into the equation.

It is the breeze of the Holy Spirit that can blow powerfully upon us and cause a vision to come alive with the life of God.

> **Ezekiel 37:9-10** - 9Also He said to me, "Prophesy to the breath, prophesy, son of man, and say to the breath, 'Thus says the Lord God: "Come from the four winds, O breath, and breathe on these slain, that they may live." ' " 10 So I prophesied as He commanded me, and breath came into them, and they lived, and stood upon their feet, an exceedingly great army.

> **John 3:8** - The wind blows where it wishes, and you hear the sound of it, but cannot tell where it comes from and where it goes. So is everyone who is born of the Spirit."

Declaration

Father, Lord, I pray for a new in-filling of the Holy Spirit in my life today. Let there be a new wave of Your revival upon my prayer life, Bible study life, and my devotion. Re-fill me with Your power and make me Your effective witness, in Jesus name.

Amen.

Day 7: Tongues of Fire

₃Then there appeared to them divided tongues, as of fire, and one sat upon each of them. ₄And they were all filled with the Holy Spirit and began to speak with other tongues, as the Spirit gave them utterance. - Acts 2:3-4

When the Holy Spirit came on the day of Pentecost, He came with a sound from heaven, as of a mighty rushing wind, that filled the whole house where they were sitting. Then all of a sudden, the disciples began to shout, pray, and praise in other tongues.

> "When this sound occurred, the multitudes came together, and were confused, because everyone heard them speak in his own language. They were all amazed and marveled, saying to one another, "Look, are not all these who speak Galileans? And how is it that we hear, each in our own language in which we were born?" – **Acts 2:6-8**

Let us not be confused when we read this because some Christians are saying, "The disciples spoke with tongues, and the people around heard and understood them. How come we speak in tongues today and people hear us but do not understand what we are speaking?"

There is a tiny difference between praying in tongues and speaking in tongues, although they're all referred to as *speaking in tongues.* In 1 Corinthians 13: 1, the Apostle Paul said, *"Even if I speak with **the tongues of men or of angels**, but have not love, I have become sounding brass or a clanging cymbal."* He understood the difference between the tongues of men and the tongues of angels.

The tongues of men are given by the Holy Spirit to be for a public sign and wonder that draws men to the Lord. That was what happened on the day of Pentecost. This still happens today. Countless reports of this manifestation in mission fields are received from time to time. The Holy Spirit empowers as He deems fit.

On the other hand, the tongues of angels are prayer languages given by the Holy Spirit to empower our prayer lives and to build up our spirits.

> **But you, beloved, building yourselves up on your most holy faith, praying in the Holy Spirit** – Jude 1:20

So yeah, it's possible to pray in tongues without speaking in tongues (other languages). Praying in tongues is for individual edification and empowerment. It enables our prayer life, helps us to be more in tune with the Holy Spirit, and opens spiritual doors of understanding to us.

> ₂ For he who speaks in a tongue does not speak to men but to God, for no one understands him; however, in the spirit he speaks mysteries. ₃ But he who prophesies speaks edification and exhortation and comfort to men. ₄ He who speaks in a tongue edifies himself, but he who prophesies edifies the church – **1 Cor. 14:2-4**

If you're a believer baptized in the Holy Spirit, continue to depend on the Holy Spirit in your prayers; every day, continue to build up your most holy faith praying in the Holy Ghost. You're not in error when you pray in tongues.

Declaration

Precious Holy Spirit, thank You for the communion that grows between You and I every day. As I seek to know You more, teach me how to pray and empower my prayer life henceforth, in Jesus name.

Amen.

Day 8: The Mantle and Healing Materials

Then he took the mantle of Elijah that had fallen from him, and struck the water, and said, "Where is the Lord God of Elijah?" And when he also had struck the water, it was divided this way and that; and Elisha crossed over. – 2 Kings 9:14

Elisha asked for a double portion of Elijah's spirit and received a mantle instead. However, the answer, the double portion he asked for, was resting on that mantle or cloak.

Jesus said that the Holy Spirit will be in you and will also be with you. That's inside and outside.

> The Spirit of truth, whom the world cannot receive because it neither sees Him nor knows Him; but you know Him, for He dwells with you and will be in you. - **John 14:17**

The power of the Holy Spirit can rest on a cloth, oil, shoes, or other materials. When the Holy Spirit's power rests on these materials, they are no longer ordinary things. Through them, God's power can be revealed and enforce great changes and miracles.

Jesus sent the apostles out with oil which they used to heal the sick.

> And they cast out many devils, and anointed with oil many that were sick, and healed them. - **Mark 6:13**

The Apostle James also told believers to use oil and pray for the sick, and they would recover.

> 14 Is anyone among you sick? Let him call for the elders of the church, and let them pray over him, anointing him with oil in the name of the Lord. 15 And the prayer of faith will save the sick, and the Lord will raise him up. And if he has committed sins, he will be forgiven. - **James 5:14-15**

And Apostle Paul also prayed over handkerchiefs and aprons, and they worked miracles.

> 11 And God gave Paul the power to do unusual miracles, 12 so that even when his

handkerchiefs or parts of his clothing were placed upon sick people, they were healed, and any demons within them came out - **Acts 19:11-12**

The power of the Holy Spirit can rest on physical materials when they are prayed over or touched by an anointed man of God. However, the faith of believers must not be on these materials, but on Jesus Christ. These materials are not the Holy Spirit. We go into error when we try to glorify these materials, monetize them, make a doctrine out of them, or make them more important than a personal relationship with God.

Mantles and healing materials are undeniably okay. They should be used as the Holy Spirit inspires and directs. However, the Holy Spirit wants to have fellowship with us. A relationship with Him is more important than these tools.

Declaration

Dear Holy Spirit, please remind me always that my fellowship and relationship with You is more important than physical tools and materials. Guide and inspire me to know when to look up to You for revelation and ideas for deliverance, healing, and a way forward. Make me dependent on You and not on physical materials and things, in Jesus name.

Amen.

Day 9: He Will Help You

Do not cast me away from Your presence, and do not take Your Holy Spirit from me. -
Psalm 51:11

This should be the daily heart cry of every believer. Why? Because the Holy Spirit is the greatest asset of the Christian. He is here to help us become the best of what God has called us to be. Jesus said:

> 15 "If you love Me, keep My commandments. 16 And I will pray the Father, and He will give you another Helper, that He may abide with you forever— 17 the Spirit of truth, whom the world cannot receive, because it neither sees Him nor knows Him; but you know Him, for **He dwells with you and will be in you.** 18 I will not leave you orphans; I will come to you." – John 14:15-18

Notice that without the Holy Spirit, we will be like orphans – helpless, and tossed about in a wicked world. But thank God for Him. He is our helper. Our comforter.

A helper is more like an assistant, a partner, an associate. This person is assigned to assist and support you so that your work will be easier, so that you will achieve better results.

But unlike human assistants, the Holy Spirit is not your subordinate. He is rather to be the senior partner. He is to give you ideas, instructions, and direction on what to do. Unfortunately, that's not how we have treated him. We relegate him to the background, and at best, we give him orders of what to do. We say, "Holy Spirit, do this." "Holy Spirit, do that." "Holy Spirit, go, and do this."

That's not how it works. We are the ones to say, "Holy Spirit, what should I do in this situation. Guide me."

Then we wait, listen, pay attention, and discern what to do. And as we commit ourselves to it, miracles happen.

The Bible says, *"I will lift up my eyes to the hills— from whence comes my help? My help comes from the Lord, Who made heaven and earth* (Psalm 121:1-2)

We do not need to be frustrated and confused every time. We can depend on the Holy Spirit to help us navigate the uncertain waters of life.

When situations crop up, call upon the Holy Spirit first. Human helpers are limited. They are not always there 247. But the Holy Spirit is ever-present, waiting for your recognition and fellowship.

Declaration

Today, Holy Spirit, I call on You to be my helper in every aspect of life. I'm sorry for relegating You to the background before now. I humbly ask You to be my Senior partner going forward. Provide me with instructions, ideas, and directions on how to become a better person and fulfill God's assignment for my life daily, in Jesus name.

Amen.

Day 10: He Will Teach You

But the Helper, the Holy Spirit, whom the Father will send in My name, He will teach you all things, and bring to your remembrance all things that I said to you. –
John 14:26

Jesus made two points here:

1.   The Holy Spirit will teach you, and

2.   He will remind you of the Word of God.

Before we look at how the Holy Spirit likely does this in our lives, let's get this settled: Jesus is not saying that we don't need teachers or that we shouldn't go to school anymore. Of course, we need to be taught. We need to read, submit to teachers, and learn.

However, Jesus is saying that even though we have teachers, the Holy Spirit is the better teacher. **No teacher teaches all things; only the Holy Spirit does.** So while we look up to our teachers, we must depend on the Holy Spirit to take us beyond the knowledge our teachers provide us. The Psalmist wrote:

> 97 Oh, how I love Your law! It is my meditation all the day. 98 You, through Your commandments, make me wiser than my enemies; for they are ever with me.

> 99 I have more understanding than all my teachers, for Your testimonies are my meditation.

> 100 I understand more than the ancients because I keep Your precepts. – Ps. 100:97-100

In my tribe, there's a proverb that says, *"Wisdom resides with old age."* Unfortunately, that's not always true.

The Psalmist, most likely David, had more understanding than all his teachers and more knowledge than the ancients (older people) in his time because the Holy Spirit taught him.

It's only the Holy Spirit who teaches a man how to kill a giant with five smooth stones, teaches him how to kill a lion without a weapon, and a bear with mere hands. You won't learn that in any college.

How to Let the Holy Spirit Teach You

If only believers let the Holy Spirit teach them, we would be the greatest inventors, writers, technocrats, and leaders of all time. Why? Because ... *"Eye has not seen, nor ear heard, nor have entered into the heart of man the things which God has prepared for those who love Him. But God has revealed them to us through His Spirit. For the Spirit searches all things, yes, the deep things of God"* (1 Cor. 2:9-10).

We can be taught by the Holy Spirit to understand the things of God that are beyond the reach of experience or human intelligence. The Holy Spirit can give us entirely new knowledge that is not found anywhere, a knowledge that creates progress and empowers others. Such knowledge can come through dreams, visions, ideas, or inspired thoughts. This is how inventions and new projects are born.

Learn to call and rely on the Holy Spirit as your teacher. He will not only teach you new things, He will also enlighten and give you a better understanding of what you learn from human teachers.

The Holy Spirit also teaches us the Word of God as we read and meditate on what we are reading. He will bring other scriptures that explain the scriptures we are trying to understand so that we will get the best out of our Bible lessons.

When someone is teaching, preaching, or sharing, the Holy Spirit will inspire the words in our hearts and cause us to hear beyond what the speaker is saying. He will pick the words and amplify them in our hearts, give us deeper meanings, and instruct our hearts for the right actions.

The teaching ministry of the Holy Spirit is incredible. We need it daily to keep away from errors, false teachings, and human-made innuendos that don't add value to our lives.

Declaration

Holy Spirit, I call upon You to be my teacher, henceforth. When I read, study, or listen, Lord, open my eyes to see beyond the letters and words. Let my spirit receive the right instructions that will keep me in Your light constantly, in Jesus name.

Amen.

Day 11: He Will Remind You

But the Helper, the Holy Spirit, whom the Father will send in My name, He will teach you all things, and bring to your remembrance all things that I said to you. –
John 14:26

Yesterday, we talked about the Holy Spirit as our teacher. When we learn to surrender to Him daily, to teach us, our lives will get better and become more productive.

The Holy Spirit is also our reminder. He will remind us of things we have forgotten when they are needed. He brings the Scriptures that we have read or heard to our remembrance so that we know what to answer or how to respond in the situation before us.

The Bible hints us of some situations where this would be needed.

Luke 12:11-12 - ₁₁ "Now when they bring you to the synagogues and magistrates and authorities, do not worry about how or what you should answer, or what you should say.

₁₂ For the Holy Spirit will teach you in that very hour what you ought to say."

Matt. 10:18-20 - ₁₈ You will be brought before governors and kings for My sake, as a testimony to them and to the Gentiles.

₁₉ But when they deliver you up, do not worry about how or what you should speak. For it will be given to you in that hour what you should speak; ₂₀ for it is not you who speak, but the Spirit of your Father who speaks in you.

Apart from the early disciples, many Christians today, especially in hostile nations, experience the situations Jesus painted here. Jesus says we shouldn't worry when we face these frightening conditions. The Holy Spirit will be right there to inspire us with the right scriptures to use and stand upon while defending our faith. He will remind us of scriptures we are to stand upon while facing our accusers.

For Christians who may not encounter such life-threatening situations, there will still be all kinds of events in our lives every day where we will need the ministry of the Holy Spirit to remind us what to say or how to respond. Maybe you are thinking of the best way to share Christ with an atheist or a new neighbor. Perhaps your child is becoming very hostile and believes you don't love her. Or perhaps you are going through a really tough time in your marriage, and you don't know what words to use and speak to your spouse. You can always depend on the Holy Spirit for what to say or how to respond.

If the Holy Spirit will help us in the terrifying settings, how much more do we need to depend on Him in less frightening situations.

Declaration

Holy Spirit, I bring before the present situation in my life right now (mention the situation)*. Please teach me what to say, how to respond, and how to navigate through this situation. Remind me scriptures I must stand upon as I depend on You for victory and breakthrough, in Jesus name.*

Amen.

Day 12: He Will Guide You

₁₂"I still have many things to say to you, but you cannot bear them now. ₁₃However, when He, the Spirit of truth, has come, He will guide you into all truth; for He will not speak on His own authority, but whatever He hears He will speak; and He will tell you things to come. - John 16:12-13

What should I do with my life? How do I know if this is the right career or job? Should I accept this proposal? Should I employ this person? What about the investment and business opportunities that are presented to me? Which ones should I invest in?

Should I send my child to this school or the other one? Should I travel out of the country? Where do we go for holiday? Should I relocate? Where should we establish our business or ministry?

Our lives are full of an endless circle of choices and decisions. How do we know we have made the right choice? Is there a mirror to gaze and be sure what we chose to do would turn out all right? Can we depend on God to guide us? How do we know that we are doing God's plan and not ours?

These are among the many questions that becloud our lives daily. Thankfully, God's Word assures:

> **"I will instruct you, says the Lord, and guide you along the best path for your life; I will counsel you and watch your progress. Don't be like a senseless horse or mule that has to have a bit in its mouth to keep it in line!** - Psalm 32:8-9 (TLB)

God will guide us and help us make the right decisions. He knows that we are incapable of determining what's best for us, hence the gift of the Holy Spirit.

You can depend on the Holy Spirit to guide you in life because it's one of His missions to us. You do not need to depend on guesswork; neither do you need to consult horoscope to know what to do as you face the myriads of choices before you. You need a guide.

A guide is someone who shows others the way because he knows the way. And who else, if not the Holy Spirit, knows the way? As Jesus said, He is here to guide us. The Scripture says:

There is a way that seems right to a man, but its end is the way of death - Proverbs 14:12).

This means that planning your life without divine input is very risky. It can lead to death. Come to the Holy Spirit when you need guidance and ask Him for direction. He will surely guide you.

The Holy Spirit will guide you into all truth. He will give you the discernment to judge between true and false teachings. He will guide you and prevent you from straying from the truth. He will guide you in the path of righteousness, and lead you to a place of fulfillment

Declaration

"Heavenly Father, I declare today that I've had enough of following my own ways. Holy Spirit, please show me Your ways, and teach me Your paths. Lead me in Your truth and guide me in the way You have ordained for me, as I seek You daily, in Jesus name.

Note: Today, bring before the Holy Spirit every plan before you and ask for His guidance in making the right choices.

Day 13: He Will Show You Things to Come

*"However, when He, the Spirit of truth, has come, He will guide you into all truth; for He will not speak on His own authority, but whatever He hears He will speak; and **He will tell you things to come.** - John 16:13*

Is it possible to know things ahead of time? Is it possible to know what's coming before they happen?

Well, Jesus said that the Holy Spirit would tell us things to come. And sure, He does just that. But just so you know, it's not intended for self-promotion, self-marketing or forecasting, but to keep us safe.

Several times in the ministry of Jesus, He knew what the Pharisees and Sadducees were thinking, and answered them to their amazement. Sometimes he saw, in the spirit, their plans to kill him and withdrew from the town to other places.

In one instance, hostile Jewish leaders expected Him to immediately come to Lazarus' help and were waiting there to trap him. By the leading of the Holy Spirit, Jesus waited two more days after hearing of Lazarus' sickness. It must have been difficult for Jesus to abstain from rushing to Lazarus' side, but the Holy Spirit led Him to stay away because there were people there who wanted to hurt Him (see John 11:1-11).

When Jesus didn't appear after Lazarus had died, these wicked religious leaders concluded He wasn't coming, so they left. As soon as they left the town, the Holy Spirit gave Jesus the go-ahead to travel to Bethany, where He raised Lazarus from the dead. Through the leading of the Holy Spirit, He avoided a hateful confrontation with irritated religious leaders (see John 11:11-45).

Jesus was led by the Holy Spirit through precarious situations on many occasions. When religious leaders with wicked intents wanted to arrest and kill Him, He was supernaturally guided by the Spirit right through the middle of the crowd, escaping injury and harm (see Luke 4:29, 30; John 8:59; John 10:39).

The Holy Spirit gives us warnings because He knows the future! He can warn you of things to come in order to prepare you for them or to keep you safe.

The way the Holy Spirit shows us things to come is always different, depending on our nature and spiritual consecration. He chooses how best to speak to us that gets our attention.

The Holy Spirit can speak through any of the following ways:

- The inner witness
- The inner voice (of the Holy Spirit)
- Quickening verses of scripture in our hearts
- Danger check in our spirit
- Deep inner comfort in our spirit (is a green light sign)
- Visions
- Dreams
- Prophecies

If it is a dream, then He speaks to us that way. If it is through His word, then he will impress scriptures upon your heart. If it is an impression, then you will just have a knowing. He speaks to us all the time, we just have to be aware and open to Him.

Declaration

Dear Holy Spirit,

I know You are always speaking and guiding us every day to keep us safe and in Your purpose for our lives. Forgive me for straying away many times in my own plans. I declare my desire to hear and understand Your leadings clearly from time to tome. Keep my spirit-man alert to recognize You from this day forward, in Jesus name.

Amen.

Day 14: He Gives You Power

₁₅And He said to them, "Go into all the world and preach the gospel to every creature. ₁₆He who believes and is baptized will be saved; but he who does not believe will be condemned. ₁₇And these signs will follow those who believe: In My name they will cast out demons; they will speak with new tongues; ₁₈they will take up serpents; and if they drink anything deadly, it will by no means hurt them; they will lay hands on the sick, and they will recover." – Mark 16:15-18

This is what Jesus wanted His disciples to do after he went to heaven – to preach with authority, heal the sick, and cast out devils. Unfortunately, the disciples were helpless, afraid, and full of questions.

Where were they going to start from? How would they explain the things they had seen? Who would believe them? Won't the religious leaders treat them the same way they treated their master?

While Jesus was physically present with them, they preached and did a few miracles here and there and were happy. But now, He was gone. They needed something to happen, something more than the ordinary, something to assure them they would be able to carry on the assignment.

A few times, Peter and others went back to their fishing business. But their minds were more on the words of Christ. He had told them, "And behold, I am sending the promise of My Father upon you. But remain in the city until you have been clothed with power from on high."

If they would be able to do what they had been commissioned to do, they would need power. They would need someone who would be with them just as Christ was with them, only this time, this person would not be seen physically, but they would know Him.

"But you shall receive power when the Holy Spirit has come upon you, and you shall be witnesses to Me in Jerusalem, and in all Judea and Samaria, and to the end of the earth." - Acts 1:8

Finally, on the day of Pentecost, the Holy Spirit came, *"and they were all filled with the Holy Spirit and began to speak with other tongues, as the Spirit gave them utterance."* This event transformed the once helpless, fearful, and stranded people into a force the world would eventually become afraid of. They went from place to place sharing their testimony with authority, healing the sick, and casting out demons.

> For unclean spirits, crying with a loud voice, came out of many who were possessed; and many who were paralyzed and lame were healed. - **Acts 8:7**

The Holy Spirit has not only come to teach us, give us utterance, and help us in prayer. He is here to help us become effective witnesses of Christ's work. He is here to empower us to preach the Gospel with authority, heal the sick, and cast out devils.

Today, we do not have to wait for the Holy Spirit to come as it was on the day of Pentecost. At the moment of salvation, we receive the Holy Spirit who indwells us. "For by one Spirit we were all baptized into one body—whether Jews or Greeks, whether slaves or

free—and have all been made to drink into one Spirit."
(1 Corinthians 12:13)

Every believer has received the indwelling of the Holy Spirit, already baptized into the body of Christ. However, we do need to seek His empowerment, which comes through desire and "waiting prayer." Without this empowerment, that is, the baptism of the Holy Spirit, we may not be able to do what Christ has commissioned us to do.

Today, set your mind on the Holy Spirit, and ask Him for a fresh encounter. Ask Him to empower you for God's assignment for your life. Get into an intense prayer moment and stay with Him. He will do something new in your life.

Declaration

Holy Spirit,

I desire a new encounter with You this day. You know very well that I cannot fulfill God's plan for my life without Your empowerment. So I ask for a fresh touch this day. Baptize me with power from on high, and make me an effective witness for Christ, in Jesus name.

Amen.

Day 15: Spiritual Songs

"But the hour is coming, and now is, when the true worshipers will worship the Father in spirit and truth; for the Father is seeking such to worship Him." - John 4:23

Here's an idea that will change your life very quickly: Learn to worship God in the spirit.

True worship is spiritual, so we must worship God spiritually. This is not the kind of worship where we clap our hands in Church and shout, "O hallelujah! Praise God!" No. It is the type of worship where we find ourselves in tears, in deep wonder and absolute amazement of his love and power.

Most times, this type of worship is not available in Church services anymore, because we are in haste to do first, second, and third services. So you create it for God in your life.

You wake up in the midnight, or find yourself a secluded place and say, *"Holy Spirit, I want to worship in truth and in spirit this moment."* Then you begin to sing and praise God. New songs will flow from your heart, sing them back to God, and just adore Him in reverence.

Make this type of worship a regular, constant, and consistent practice. It will bring you closer to God and stir a release of His power in your life like never before. You will find yourself doing amazing things through the Holy Spirit.

> Speaking to one another in psalms and hymns and spiritual songs, ***singing and making melody in your heart to the Lord*** - Ephesians 5:19

> Let the word of Christ dwell in you richly in all wisdom, teaching and admonishing one another in psalms and hymns and spiritual songs, **singing with grace in your hearts to the Lord.** - Colossians 3:16

It's time to practice the word – singing from your spirit to the Lord.

What is the conclusion then? I will pray with the spirit, and I will also pray with the understanding. I will sing with the spirit, and I will also sing with the understanding. - 1 Corinthians 14:15

The Holy Spirit will inspire your worship, but you must create the time. We've sang with understanding for a long time; it's time to start singing in the spirit.

Action

Today, wake up in the middle of the night and spend one hour or more just worshipping God. Let the Holy Spirit stir worship in you. Sing from your spirit to the Lord.

Declaration

Holy Spirit, I willfully tune my mind and my spirit to Your service. Stir worship in my heart today and every day, in Jesus name.

Amen.

Day 16: He Will Help You in Prayers

Likewise the Spirit also helps in our weaknesses. For we do not know what we should pray for as we ought, but the Spirit Himself makes intercession for us with groanings which cannot be uttered. – Romans 8:26

Every Christian believes there is power in prayer. We regularly hear statements like:

"There is power in prayer. The level of breakthrough you'll enjoy in life is dependent on the extent you're willing to tarry in prayer."

When we hear declarations like that or listen to stories of great exploits of men through prayer, we get stirred up to pray. But the desire quickly wanes when we realize that prayer is hard. We start praying, only to get tongue-tied, with nothing more to say.

Thankfully, the Holy Spirit is available to help us in prayer. As the Scripture says:

"In the same way, the Spirit comes to us and helps us in our weakness. We do not know what prayer to offer or how to offer it as we should, but the Spirit Himself knows our need and at the right time intercedes on our behalf with sighs and groanings too deep for words.

27 And He who searches the hearts knows what the mind of the Spirit is, because the Spirit intercedes [before God] on behalf of God's people in accordance with God's will (Romans 8:26-27 AMP)".

What the Apostle Paul is saying here is simple:

- When it comes to prayer, we're all weak. So you're not alone when you get weak to pray

- We do not know what prayer to offer or how to offer it as we should in prayer

- But the Holy Spirit Himself knows our needs

- He comes to help us in our weaknesses and intercedes on our behalf

- He knows the mind of God and therefore intercedes in accordance with the will of God

Isn't that great?

The Holy Spirit will help you in prayer so that you won't have to be tongue-tied, confused, and struggle during prayers. He will help you pray according to God's will, and we know that prayers made in God's will are always answered.

So you don't have to continue to struggle in prayers. Invite the Holy Spirit and let Him help you each time you think of praying.

How Does the Holy Spirit Help Us in Prayers?

The Holy Spirit helps us in prayer by:

- *Giving us prayer burdens.* Any time you suddenly get burdened to pray, leave everything, go and pray. That's the Holy Spirit telling you that prayer is needed at this time.

- *Bringing into our minds things and areas to pray for.* When you start praying, the Holy Spirit will try to guide you towards different areas or persons to pray for. Don't argue, just obey.

- *Making you sad without any reason.* When you suddenly become sad, and there is no reason for that, that's the Holy Spirit communicating with you that you need to come to a place of prayer at that time.

- *Enabling us to pray in the language of the Spirit.* When we pray in tongues, we are praying in the Holy Spirit. Release yourself to the Holy Spirit during prayers and pray in the Spirit as He gives you utterance.

- *Gives us visions while in prayer.* You will suddenly see things in your mind's eye during prayers. Note them because that's the Holy Spirit speaking and guiding you.

How Do We Get the Holy Spirit Into Our Prayer?

Note that the Holy Spirit won't do the praying for you while you lay down sleeping. You will be the one praying. The Holy Spirit helps you.

To get the Holy Spirit to help you in prayer:

- Call him to come and assist you when you want to pray

- Start praying, knowing in faith, that He is going to take over

- Pray in the Holy Spirit

- Express out songs, prayer words, or thoughts the Holy suddenly brings into your spirit.

Let the Holy Spirit empower your prayer life henceforth.

Declaration

Dear Holy Spirit,

I recognize that You help us in our infirmities. You help us in prayer and help us please God in our prayers.

Today, and always, I surrender my mind, intellect, and desires to You. I ask that You empower my prayer life from this moment onwards, in Jesus name.

Amen.

Day 17: The Fruit of the Holy Spirit

₂₂But the fruit of the Spirit is love, joy, peace, longsuffering, kindness, goodness, faithfulness, ₂₃gentleness, self-control. Against such there is no law. - Galatians 5:22-23

The fruit of the Holy Spirit are God's characteristics produced in the life of the believer by the Holy Spirit. The Scripture lists them as love, joy, peace, longsuffering, kindness, goodness, faithfulness, gentleness, and self-control. As humans, these qualities are not always easy to grow without help. But with the Holy Spirit in us, we can manifest them every day because, in truth, we are not the ones bearing the fruit; it is the Holy Spirit in us who bears the fruit.

A Christian can rely on the Holy Spirit to love even in the most difficult moments, be joyful even when there is no reason to, have peace in troublous times, be patient when there is no need to, and exercise self-control. Why? Because the Holy Spirit bears these fruit in our lives, not we trying to work out some great qualities.

However, just as natural fruit needs time to nurture, the fruit of the Holy Spirit will not mature in our lives overnight. As every successful gardener must fight against weeds to enjoy the fruit they desire, we must continually work to get rid of the "weeds" of our old self that always strives to gag the work of the Holy Spirit in us.

- You can love no matter the circumstances

- You can be joyful even when things seems messed up

- You can have peace even in very troublous times

- You can be tolerant, forgiving, and patient even with the most venomous person on earth

- You can be good, faithful, and gentle, both with yourself and with others notwithstanding all the negative conditions and reasons not to be

- You can have self-control so that you're free from every negative addiction

The Holy Spirit is the Seed that produces these qualities. He is already in us. All we need to do is let Him and depend on Him to work out these fruit in our lives. As we give Him more control of our lives every day, He begins to do in us and through us what only He can do – shaping us and molding us to look like Jesus.

> 17 Now the Lord is the Spirit; and where the Spirit of the Lord is, there is liberty. 18 But we all, with unveiled face, beholding as in a mirror the glory of the Lord, are being transformed into the same image from glory to glory, just as by the Spirit of the Lord. - 2 Corinthians 3:17-18

Declaration

Heavenly Father,

Thank You for engrafting me in Christ Jesus by the Holy Spirit as a branch. You designed me to bear fruit of righteousness, love, peace, joy, gentleness, self-control, goodness, patience, and kindness.

O Lord, I desire to bear these fruits in my life henceforth,

Holy Spirit, I desire to remain rooted in Christ, bearing fruit that leads others to the light of God's love. I desire to walk in LOVE, forgiving others at all times and gifting God's blessings on my life with others, just as God Loved and gave Jesus to die for us.

I desire, every day, to walk in joy, peace, gentleness, self-control, goodness, patience, and kindness so that I will be an example that brings others to Christ. Help me, empower me, and teach me to bear Your fruit every day, in Jesus name. Amen.

Day 18: Why Bear the Fruit of the Spirit?

43"For a good tree does not bear bad fruit, nor does a bad tree bear good fruit. 44For every tree is known by its own fruit. For men do not gather figs from thorns, nor do they gather grapes from a bramble bush. 45A good man out of the good treasure of his heart brings forth good; and an evil man out of the evil treasure of his heart brings forth evil. For out of the abundance of the heart his mouth speaks. - Luke 6:43-45

Today's scripture is very easy to follow:

- Apple trees will not produce maize fruits; neither will a lion give birth to a goat.

- So if we do not bear the fruit of the Holy Spirit, how are we going to explain to people that we have the Holy Spirit?

Speaking in tongues is great, fasting and praying is magnificent, but without the fruit of the Spirit in our lives, we can't demonstrate that we have the Holy Spirit. So we must desire and invest our consciousness with the Holy Spirit, and let Him develop His fruit in our lives.

The Apostle Peter said:

> ₅But also for this very reason, giving all diligence, add to your faith virtue, to virtue knowledge, ₆ to knowledge self-control, to self-control perseverance, to perseverance godliness, ₇ to godliness brotherly kindness, and to brotherly kindness love.

> ₈For if these things are yours and abound, you will be neither barren nor unfruitful in the knowledge of our Lord Jesus Christ.

> ₉For he who lacks these things is shortsighted, even to blindness, and has forgotten that he was cleansed from his old sins. - 2 Peter 1:5-9

If we don't bear the fruit of the spirit, we will bear the fruit of the flesh, which will make our Christianity void of positive results. Bearing the fruit of the flesh will make us unproductive. Jesus said that every tree will be known by the fruits it bears and that by their fruits, we shall know them.

The fruit of the Holy Spirit is:

- The key to answered prayer (John 15:16).

- The key to favor with God.

- The key to angelic protection.

- The key to God's mercy

- The key to divine health (Proverbs 17:22)

- The key to long life (1 Peter 3:8-12; Psalm 34:8-18)

- The key to character

- The key to standing out in life.

- The key to influencing others positively

- The key to a good marriage and relationship

You can command all the devils in the universe, or chain all the witches and wizards in Bermuda Triangle, but if you don't show the fruit of the Holy Spirit, you won't go very far in life. It is the fruit of the Holy Spirit that opens every door.

Declaration

Today, Holy Spirit, I once again express my desire to manifest Your fruit of love, joy, peace, longsuffering, kindness, goodness, faithfulness, gentleness, and self-control

Provide me with daily assistance to bear these fruits in abundance, so that Jesus will be glorified in my life every day.

Make me an example in character and in everything so that I could win the race set before me and not be a cast away after preaching to others, in Jesus name

Amen

Day 19: How to Bear the Fruit of the Spirit

₅But also for this very reason, giving all diligence, add to your faith virtue, to virtue knowledge, ₆to knowledge self-control, to self-control perseverance, to perseverance godliness, ₇to godliness brotherly kindness, and to brotherly kindness love. - 2 Pet 1:5-7

If I desire to grow an apple fruit, I won't do it by just talking. I would need to find the right soil, plant the seed, and nurture it. The process takes time, requires knowledge and diligence.

We have received the Holy Spirit who lives in us; He is the repository of God's nature and fruit of righteousness. To grow the fruit of the Holy Spirit in us, we must cultivate them. And to cultivate them requires knowledge and diligence – that is, hard work.

The Scripture said, *"Therefore, brethren, be even more diligent to make your call and election sure, for if you do these things you will never stumble; for so an entrance will be supplied to you abundantly into the everlasting kingdom of our Lord and Savior Jesus Christ"* (2 Pet 1:10-11).

Yes, the fruit of the Spirit is the work of the Holy Spirit in us, but we need to make room for them to grow. We need to cultivate the fruit and tend to them. How do you do that?

Define Your Association: Ungodly association hinders spiritual growth and development. If the people with whom you relate with daily are those that mock the things of God and given to gluttony, then you're sure to be like them. Their relationship will resist the growth of the fruit of the Spirit in you.

Feed your spirit man. God's word is the food of the Holy Spirit. Feed on it daily and be full of it always. It will provide the nutrients for the fruit of the Holy Spirit in you to grow.

Meditate on the Word. Your life moves in the direction of your deepest thoughts. What enters your heart has entered your life, and will affect your behavior. When it sinks in, it becomes your nature.

Practice daily devotion: A daily fellowship with the Lord, exposing yourself to God's presence every day, empowers the fruit of the Spirit in you to grow.

Cast your cares on the Lord. When you focus on the cares of the world, it will choke your spirit from bearing fruit. Learn to "be anxious for nothing, but in everything by prayer and supplication, with thanksgiving, let your requests be made known to God; and the peace of God, which surpasses all understanding, will guard your hearts and minds through Christ Jesus (Philippians 4:6-8)

Fellowship with other believers. Don't be like some Christians who say that they serve God in their house, depending on online messages and write-ups only. The Bible admonishes us not to abstain from the gathering of believers. Join other Christians in fellowship regularly. Be involved in a church where your spirit is stirred regularly towards a commitment to God and prayers.

Be open to correction. Submit to spiritual leadership that strives to bring out the best in you, one that will correct, challenge, and inspire you on to deeper encounter with God. If a child does not have correct parenting, he is never held accountable; therefore he turns out wrong.

Continually Pray for the Fruit of the Spirit. Consistently put the Lord in remembrance to help you grow the fruit of the Spirit. Prayer is the rain that waters our soil and makes it yield.

Declaration

O Lord,

Please show me, every day, what I must do to let the fruit of the Spirit develop in me, in Jesus name.

Amen.

Day 20: Prayers for the Fruit of the Spirit

"For the fruit of the Spirit is in all goodness and righteousness and truth." - Ephesians 5:9

Dedicate today and pray for the fruit of the Holy Spirit. Talk to Him all through the day, and ask Him to manifest His fruit in your life. According to Galatians 5:22-23, the fruit of the Holy Spirit include:

- Love,
- Joy,
- Peace,
- Forbearance (Longsuffering, Patience),
- Kindness,
- Goodness,
- Faithfulness,
- Gentleness
- Self-control

When these are in abundance in our lives, we produce results for the Kingdom of God, receive His promises, overcome the devil daily, and win in all situations.

Meditate on these prayers and say them in your heart to God all through the day. When you're a going to bed, make out time to pray the prayers.

Prayers

1. Heavenly Father, Thank You for engrafting me in Christ Jesus by the Holy Spirit as a branch.

You designed me to bear fruits of righteousness, love, peace, joy, gentleness, self-control, goodness, patience, and kindness.

O LORD, I desire to bear these fruits in my life henceforth, in Jesus name.

---

2. Dear Holy Spirit, I desire to remain rooted in Christ, bearing fruits that lead others to the light of God's love.

I desire to walk in LOVE, forgiving others at all times and gifting God's blessings on my life with others, just as God Loved and gave Jesus to die for us.

I desire to walk in joy every day of my life, thereby drawing from the well of salvation.

Please remind and help me at all times to LOVE and be joyful as I live, in Jesus name.

---

3. Holy Spirit, I desire to walk in peace with myself and with others as a child of God.

I desire to walk in patience, for faith makes no haste.

I desire to walk in kindness, thoughtfulness, and compassion for others just as Christ was compassionate at all times.

Provide me with daily assistance to bear these fruits of peace, patience, and kindness in abundance, so that Jesus will be glorified in my life every day, in Jesus name.

---

4. Holy Spirit, I desire to bear the fruit of Goodness, so that I may lead others to Jesus Christ.

I desire to be faithful at all times with whatever God blesses me with, so that I may stand before God in the end and receive the rewards of faithfulness.

I desire to be gentle with myself and others, in thoughts, words, and actions, so that I may be an instrument of encouragement and uplifting to others and not discouragement.

I desire to walk in Self-control in food, dressing, and in everything so that I could win the race set before me and not be a cast away after preaching to others.

I call upon You to empower me every day to bear these fruits as I live, serve God, and relate with others, in Jesus name, I pray.

Amen.

Day 21: Five Wonders of the Holy Spirit

₃₈ Then Peter said to them, "Repent, and let every one of you be baptized in the name of Jesus Christ for the remission of sins; and you shall receive the gift of the Holy Spirit. ₃₉ For the promise is to you and to your children, and to all who are afar off, as many as the Lord our God will call." - Acts 2:38-39

The promise of the Holy Spirit is to you and to your children, and to all who are afar off, as many as the Lord our God will call. If you are a believer, you have received the Holy Spirit in you (see John 14:16-17).

Today, let's see five more of the works of the Holy Spirit in our lives. This is what I call the five wonders of the Holy Spirit

1. He Indwells Us

=> **Scripture:** ₉ But you are not in the flesh but in the Spirit, if indeed the Spirit of God dwells in you. Now if anyone does not have the Spirit of Christ, he is not His. ₁₀ And if Christ is in you, the body is dead because of sin, but the Spirit is life because of righteousness. ₁₁ But if the Spirit of Him who raised Jesus from the dead dwells in you, He who raised Christ from the dead will also give life to your mortal bodies through His Spirit who dwells in you. - Romans 8:9-11

=> **Comment:** The indwelling of the Holy Spirit means that God now lives in us by the Holy Spirit. We may not understand the wonder, but we can accept it because that's what the Word says.

The indwelling of God's Spirit also means that our hearts and our bodies are a sanctuary for God, and we should treat and use our bodies accordingly.

=> **Declaration:** *My Body is the temple of the Holy Spirit. God lives in me through the Holy Spirit. Because I am God's habitation, I am clean, undefiled, and accepted in the beloved.*

---

2. He Renews Us

=> **Scripture:** ₄ But when the kindness and the love of God our Savior toward man appeared, ₅ not by works of righteousness which we have done, but according to His mercy *He saved us, through the washing of regeneration and renewing of the Holy Spirit,* ₆ whom He poured out on us abundantly through Jesus Christ our Savior. - Titus 3:4-6

=> **Comment:** We are born again by the Holy Spirit. We now have a new life in us. The Holy Spirit renews us every day. Even if our outward man is perishing, the Holy Spirit renews our inward man day-by-day (2Corinthians 4:16).

=> **Declaration:** *I am renewed by the Holy Spirit every day. I am empowered in my spirit every day. I am being made more Holy every day. I am getting better every day.*

---

3. He Baptizes Us

=> **Scripture:** "For I will pour water on him who is thirsty, and floods on the dry ground; I will pour My Spirit on your descendants, and My blessing on your offspring. - Isaiah 44:3

=> **Comment:** The outpouring of the Spirit is different from the indwelling of the Spirit. The Holy

Spirit comes to indwell us at salvation. The outpouring of the Spirit is the baptism of the Holy Spirit that empowers the gifts of the Holy Spirit in us.

=> **Declaration:** *Dear Holy Spirit, I desire a new and deeper encounter with You every day. I desire Your baptism that empowers me to be an effective witness of Christ, in Jesus name*

---

4. He Leads Us

=> **Scripture:** For as many as are led by the Spirit of God, these are sons of God. - Romans 8:14

=> **Comment:** Without daily guidance and direction we will fall into the dangers and traps of the enemy. Thankfully, the Holy Spirit is available to lead and guide us in our day-to-day dealings. All we have to do is trust Him, rely on Him, and call on Him to guide us in everything.

=> **Declaration:** *Thank You Holy Spirit for being our guide and instructor. I want You to know that I trust Your guidance and daily leadings. Please continue to guide me, in Jesus name.*

5. He Seals Us

=>***Scripture:*** ₁₃ In Him you also trusted, after you heard the word of truth, the gospel of your salvation; in whom also, having believed, you were sealed with the Holy Spirit of promise, ₁₄ who is the guarantee of our inheritance until the redemption of the purchased possession, to the praise of His glory. - Ephesians 1:13-14

=> ***Comment:*** A seal is like a stamp indicating who owns the goods or property. The Holy Spirit in us is God's stamp that we are saved and have an inheritance in His Kingdom.

=> **Declaration:** *I am sealed with the Holy Spirit. I am a child of God. My salvation is certain. I have an inheritance in God's kingdom.*

Day 22: Understanding Spiritual Gifts

₆Having then gifts differing according to the grace that is given to us, let us use them: if prophecy, let us prophesy in proportion to our faith; ₇or ministry, let us use it in our ministering; he who teaches, in teaching; ₈he who exhorts, in exhortation; he who gives, with liberality; he who leads, with diligence; he who shows mercy, with cheerfulness. – **Rom. 12: 6-8**

Spiritual gifts are supernatural abilities given to individual believers by the Holy Spirit for edification of the Church. They can also be God's natural abilities that function through the direction of the Holy Spirit. Gifts such as healing, speaking in tongues, miracles, and prophecy, are supernatural, while gifts such as administration, helps, and teaching are natural. Though in the world, people may have same natural abilities, they do not function under the direction of the Holy Spirit. The Holy Spirit gives and uses these abilities for His purposes in the lives of believers.

Spiritual gifts are given by the Holy Spirit freely. We do not receive it because we prayed and fasted for a hundred days. If you didn't have one ability already given to you by the Holy Spirit, even if you prayed non-stop for 365 days, that particular gift won't manifest in your life. Fasting and prayer only stir the gifts we have already received.

Our major role in the spiritual gifts conversation is to know what they are and discover the ones already given to us by the Holy Spirit.

> *You don't fast and pray to receive spiritual gifts; you only fast and pray to discover and stir your spiritual gifts.*

Your spiritual gifts are not the same as your natural talents. Your natural talents are skills you were born with or skills you learned as you go through life, while spiritual gifts are given to you by the Holy Spirit at salvation and baptism of the Holy Spirit.

This means that your natural talents are still useful. They are designed for your physical profiting, while spiritual gifts are designed primarily for kingdom profiting.

As we delve into this study, therefore, let us desire to learn what gifts the Holy Spirit has bestowed on us and pray for their manifestation, so that we may *"according to the grace that is given to us, use them; if prophecy, let us prophesy in proportion to our faith; or ministry, let us use it in our ministering; he who teaches, in teaching; he who exhorts, in exhortation; he who gives, with liberality; he who leads, with diligence; he who shows mercy, with cheerfulness."*

Declaration

Heavenly Father,

I ask that You open my understanding to recognize and accept the spiritual gifts in me by the Holy Spirit. Give me undeniable signs that point to these abilities designed to make me bear fruits for Your kingdom, in Jesus name

Amen.

Day 23: The Purpose of Spiritual Gifts

Now to each one the manifestation of the Spirit is given for the common good. - 1 Corinthians 12:7

God is a God of purpose. When the purpose of God for a thing is not known, abuse is inevitable. The parable of Jesus on talents shows that a day of reckoning is coming. Even though the parable teaches on physical talents, abilities, and investments, the lessons also apply for spiritual gifts. So what are God's purposes for spiritual gifts?

1. For the Common Good

As the scripture says, *"the manifestation of the Spirit is given for the common good."* Other translations put it this way:

- The Holy Spirit displays God's power through each of us as a means of helping the entire church (TLB).

- A spiritual gift is given to each of us so we can help each other (NLV).

- The Spirit has given each of us a special way of serving others (CEV).

Spiritual gifts are for the building up and edification of the body of Christ – the local church. It is not for the profiting of the person with the gift. All display of spiritual gifts must be done to bring glory to God.

Even so, you, since you are zealous for spiritual gifts, let it be for the edification of the church that you seek to excel. - 1 Cor. 14:12

Your spiritual gifts are for the service of the local church where you belong. So if you don't belong to a local church, that's the first error. You need to find one, belong there, and let your gifts serve others.

The problem usually arises when the person with the gift begins to demand more attention than necessary. This is why many pastors refuse to teach and acknowledge the manifestation of spiritual gifts in their assembly. But it doesn't have to be so.

Kenneth Hagin (Snr) wrote, *"I'd rather have a little wildfire than have no fire at all."* Instead of discouraging and refusing the manifestation of spiritual gifts, let us teach the Church how to use the gifts orderly and for the profiting of the body as God expects.

2. For God's Glory

Everything God does is for His praise. He empowers us with spiritual gifts so that His glory will be seen among us.

> **These people I have formed for Myself;**
> **they shall declare My praise.** - Isaiah 43:21

It is an abuse of spiritual gifts if God is not being projected and glorified through the gifts. We must never come to that point where we think that we have the power to do anything. God is the One doing everything through us for His glory. When we don't return all glory to Him, we are setting ourselves up for disaster.

The donkey that carried Jesus walked on red carpet. However, it was not to it people were spreading their garments, but so long as He was carrying Christ, He was being honored. Imagine if the donkey felt he was the one people were clapping for.

We must glorify God with our gifts.

3. A Way to Convict Sinners

The sinner's heart is, many times, hardened by the devil. It takes spiritual impartation to humble their heart and lead them to Christ's love.

> 24 But if all prophesy, and an unbeliever or an uninformed person comes in, he is convinced by all, he is convicted by all. 25 And thus the secrets of his heart are revealed; and so, falling down on his face, he will worship God and report that God is truly among you. - 1 Corinthians 14:24-25

Imagine if our churches manifest the gifts of healing, word of knowledge, prophecy, power, miracles, and faith. No doubt, we won't find it hard getting sinners saved and filling the pews.

In Mathew 16:18, Jesus says that He will build His church and the gates of hell shall not prevail against it. Spiritual gifts are among the tools God uses to build His Church.

Declaration

Dear Holy Spirit, show me my spiritual gifts and empower their manifestation in my life for the Glory of God, in Jesus name.

Amen.

Day 24: Types of Spiritual Gifts (1): Utterance Gifts

₈for to one is given the word of wisdom through the Spirit, to another the word of knowledge through the same Spirit, ₉to another faith by the same Spirit, to another gifts of healings by the same Spirit, ₁₀to another the working of miracles, to another prophecy, to another discerning of spirits, to another different kinds of tongues, to another the interpretation of tongues. ₁₁But one and the same Spirit works all these things, distributing to each one individually as He wills. - 1 Corinthians 12:8-11

There are nine spiritual gifts as stated in the scripture mentioned above, namely: word of wisdom, word of knowledge, faith, healing, working of miracles, prophecy, discerning of spirits, divers kinds of tongues and interpretation of tongues. These gifts are classified into three, namely: utterance gifts, power gifts, and wisdom gift.

The Holy Spirit gives spiritual gifts to us, according to His will. Though He may give two people the same gift, the gift may operate differently in them. It is called diversities of operations.

Utterance Gifts

- Speaking in tongues
- Interpretation of tongues
- Prophecy

Power Gift

- Faith
- Gift of healing
- Discerning of spirit

Wisdom Gift

- Gift of word of wisdom
- Gift of word of knowledge
- Gift of discerning of spirit

Today, let's talk about the utterance gifts.

1. Speaking In Tongues

Speaking in tongues is a spiritual expression of a believer in unknown tongues or words that cannot be understood. The gift of unknown tongues is known as diversities of tongues because there is a tongue of men and tongues of an angel.

The tongues of men is when you are speaking a word that is not known to you, but someone else understands it because it is his native language. This is when someone by the help of the Holy Spirit is speaking a native language of another person which he has no foreknowledge of.

The tongues of angel are when you are speaking a language that is not an earthly language which can only be understood through the gift of the interpretation of tongues.

There are three ways this gift of unknown tongues can be expressed. It can be expressed in speaking which is also classified with prophecy (1 Corinthians 14:4-6); it can be expressed in prayer (1 Corinthians 14:14-16), and it can be expressed in songs (Ephesians 5:19, 1 Corinthians 14:15).

Speaking in tongues is a spiritual gift for the edification of the body of Christ. However, if there is no interpreter, the words that were spoken would be profitless.

If God gives a message to the church through you and you delivered it through speaking in tongues, nobody will benefit from that message except there is an interpreter.

But when you are praying or singing in tongues, you are praying and singing to the Lord; therefore, it does not require interpretation.

Speaking in tongues is not a language that should be learned or taught because it is a gift of the Holy Spirit, but it can be desired. Our Lord Jesus Christ said that those that hunger and thirst after righteousness shall be satisfied.

2. Interpretation of Tongues

This gift enables the receiver to be able to decode and interpret the unknown tongues when they are spoken.

There have been a few times that someone delivered a message in tongues and someone interpreted what was said. Like every other gift, this gift is highly needed in the body of Christ today.

3. Prophecy

Prophecy is a supernatural ability to give a message from God in a language that can be understood. It is the ability to declare the mind of God to a person or group of persons. This gift gives you the ability to speak on behalf of God.

Prophecy can come from a preacher or teacher while they are preaching and declaring the word of God. Prophecy can also come from you while reading scriptures, worshipping God, or meditating on the Word. It can also occur through visions, dreams or trances.

There are three areas to consider when it comes to prophecy:

a) **How Old Testament Prophets Worked**: The Old Testament prophets were used by God to inform and warn the nation of impending judgment and to reveal God's blessings for obedience, and the coming of God's Kingdom. They were foretelling, predicting, and forecasting future events.

b) **How New Testament Prophets Worked**: New Testament prophets typically spoke the mind of God to the Church, with some exceptions where Prophet Agabus foretold a drought (Acts 11:27-28) and Paul's imprisonment (Acts 21:10-14). New Testament prophets do not typically foretell events. They *"forthtell"* God's word, that is, they reveal the mind of God for the moment.

c) **The gift of Prophecy:** There are those with prophetic grace, called into the ministry as prophets. These people will likely prophesy more often than others, and carry on ministry assignments as prophets. But others may have only the gift of prophecy without being called into the ministry as prophets. One can prophesy without necessarily being a prophet.

On occasions, today's prophet may see future events. While it's not always the case, it's not unlikely. Those with the gift of prophecy will most likely give messages that encourage, reassure and inspire others of God's love in their lives. The most important thing, however, is that we don't force ourselves to do anything. We must surrender to the Holy Spirit and let Him use us.

The Apostle Paul believes that the gift of prophecy has greater value in the Church than the gift of tongues.

> 2 For he who speaks in a tongue does not speak to men but to God, for no one understands him; however, in the spirit he speaks mysteries. 3 But he who prophesies speaks edification and exhortation and comfort to men.

> 4 He who speaks in a tongue edifies himself, but he who prophesies edifies the church. 5 I wish you all spoke with tongues, but even more that you prophesied; for he who prophesies is greater than he who speaks with tongues, unless indeed he interprets, that the church may receive edification. - 1 Corinthians 14:2-5

However, as stated in the previous chapter, the purpose of the gift of prophecy is to build up the church and glorify Jesus Christ, not to attract attention to ourselves.

How to Judge Prophecy

Not everything that sounds like prophecy is truthfully prophecy. Some are willfully made up by folks trying to hoodwink others into an undue advantage. So we must judge prophecy to discern truth from error. The Bible says, *"Let two or three prophets speak, and let the others judge (1 Corinthians 14:29)."*

Here are questions to ask about prophecies:

- Is it in agreement with the written Word of God (Galatians 1:8)?

- Does it edify or condemn? God does not condemn us.

- Does it lead to repentance? True prophecies must lead to repentance

- What is the end goal? If it tilts towards money and seed-sowing, then it's from a wrong premise

- Who is glorified? Prophecies must glorify God and not the prophet

- Does it come to pass? If God gave the word, then it must come to pass (see Deuteronomy 18:20-22)

Declaration

O Lord,

I thank You for the clarity that Your Word brings. Thank You for the spiritual gifts in my life. Thank You for the understanding of how my gifts will bring You praise, in Jesus name.

Amen.

Day 25: Types of Spiritual Gifts (2): Power Gifts

₉to another faith by the same Spirit, to another gifts of healings by the same Spirit, ₁₀ to another the working of miracles... - 1 Corinthians 11:9-10

Yesterday we began to talk about spiritual gifts. We defined what they are and how they are divided. We talked about the utterance gifts that consist of prophecy, speaking in tongues, and interpretation of tongues. Today, let's see what the power gifts are.

4. The Gift of Faith

The Bible has a lot to say about faith. Every Christian is called upon to have faith and grow their faith. But the gift of faith is something different.

When someone is gifted with the spiritual gift of faith, they are able to believe God in the most unusual circumstances. The Holy Spirit stirs the person's spirit with unusual courage and confidence to dare what may seem impossible and to do the unimaginable.

When the spiritual gift of faith is in operation, the person may not be able to explain the reason why they believe the way they do. They may not know what they are doing or what is pushing them.

The gift of faith produces uncommon miracles. For example, while general faith will trust God for healing that happens gradually, the gift of faith will trust God for instant healing and see it happen.

At the Beautiful Gate, the Holy Spirit stirred the spirits of Peter and John with the gift of faith. They looked at the paralyzed man, and Peter said, *"Silver and gold I do not have, but what I do have I give you: In the name of Jesus Christ of Nazareth, rise up and walk* (Acts 3:6)."

When the man didn't understand what they were saying, Peter *"took him by the right hand and lifted him up, and immediately his feet and ankle bones received strength* (vs. 7)."

It was not the sick man's faith that got him healed. It was Peter and John's faith that healed the man. They were operating in the gift of faith right there.

The spiritual gift of faith brings raw power into action. Later, Peter would explain to the audience, *"His name, **through faith in His name,** has made this man strong, whom you see and know. Yes, the faith which comes through Him has given him this perfect soundness in the presence of you all."*– Acts 3:16

That man did not even know the Jesus that Peter and John was talking about when he was healed, so it was obviously not his faith that got him healed. It was the faith of Peter and his colleague, John.

If you are gifted with the spiritual gift of faith, you will find yourself, when the Holy Spirit stirs that gift, believing God for the most difficult things, and right before your eyes, you will see them happen.

5. The Gift of Healing

Just like the gift of faith, the Bible commands us to lay hands on the sick and heal them. We lay hands on the sick almost every Sunday and speak God's healing over them. We are obeying Jesus' instruction to heal the sick. And we receive great testimonies for obeying the command to lay hands on the sick and heal them.

However, with the spiritual gift of healing in operation, the healing will be more frequent and more dramatic. While there are diversities in the operation of the gift of healing, one fact to know is that a person with the gift of healing will get more results than others simply laying hands on the sick and trying to get them healed.

But we shouldn't wait until we confirm that we have the gift of healing before praying for the sick. Pray for the sick from time to time. Anoint them with oil and speak healing over them. It is Jesus' command to us. Don't wait until you think you have the gift of healing before doing that.

6. The Gift of Working of Miracles

A miracle is a divine operation that transcends what is normally perceived as natural law; it cannot be explained upon any logical basis. Miracles happen when God intervenes in our lives, and natural laws are suspended.

Do miracles still happen today?

Of course, yes. Jesus Christ is the same yesterday, today, and forever. His miracles did not end while He was on earth. His power is still active today - healing, delivering, and intervening in people's lives.

The Holy Spirit can gift individuals with the gift of miracles because God wants to work miracles in our time just as He did in the times of Moses, Elisha, Jesus, Phillip, Paul, and Peter. He will use us if we have been crucified with Christ and are letting Christ live through us.

We must not forget, however, that miracles are intended to lead people to God, not to individuals. It is also dangerous to follow after miracles because not all miracles are of God; some are of Satan and meant to deceive (2 Thessalonians 2:9).

Declaration

I believe that Jesus Christ is the same yesterday, today, and forever. I believe that the Holy Spirit is at work in my life and that my gifts will speak forth to the glory of God, in Jesus name.

Amen.

Day 26: Types of Spiritual Gifts (3): Wisdom Gifts

₈for to one is given the word of wisdom through the Spirit, to another the word of knowledge through the same Spirit. - 1Cor. 12:9

The Holy Spirit gives spiritual gifts to us, according to His will. Two people may have the same gifts, but the operation will always not be the same. Let's look at the wisdom gifts.

7. The Gift of Word of Wisdom

The gift of word of wisdom is a sudden knowing or revelation from the Holy Spirit concerning what a person should do in regards to a situation in their lives. It is the Holy Spirit revealing the mind and purpose of God regarding something in someone's life.

The gift of *word of wisdom* is not the same as the gift of wisdom. If one has received *wisdom* from God, then wisdom resides in him. Every day, he is able to make wise choices and respond to issues through the guidance of God's spirit in His heart, in such a way that others will be blessed, and recognize that he is a wise person.

But if one has the *gift of word of wisdom*, then the Holy Spirit stirs that person's spirit every so often, giving him instant details about solutions to problems in the lives of others. So while wisdom teaches you what to do and say in your life and enables you to counsel others accurately, the *word of wisdom* comes as a sudden supernatural knowing that reveals to you what someone else should do to solve a problem or handle a situation properly.

8. The Gift of Word of Knowledge

The word of wisdom and the word of knowledge are closely related. They often operate together. While knowledge involves knowing the facts, wisdom involves the application of the facts. So the gift of the word of knowledge is a revelation from the Holy that tells a person the facts of a matter, either past, present, or future.

For example, while preaching the Holy Spirit may drop a person's name in my heart, and I suddenly know the problems this person has passed through or is currently going through. That's the word of knowledge. But then, when the Holy Spirit proceeds to drop into my spirit what the person should do to resolve the situation, that's the word of wisdom.

Some examples:

Joseph interpreted Pharaoh's dream concerning the coming years of plenty and drought - that's the word of knowledge. But then, he gives direction on how to prepare for it – that's the word of wisdom (Genesis 41:1-36).

Jesus tells his disciples how they would find the servant – that's the word of knowledge. But he also tells them what to do and how to prepare for the Passover – that's the word of wisdom (Mark 14:12-15).

One thing to note about the gifts of the word of wisdom and word of knowledge is that you do not preplan these things. You do not come prepared to tell people some stuff you got to know about them through information. The Holy Spirit gives you these details suddenly, while waiting on Him in a place of prayer, or while preaching the word. These revelations can come as:

- Inner impressions

- The inner witness of the Holy Spirit

- Inner pictures and movie-like scenes

- Revelation of scriptures

- Dreams and visions

- Angelic visitations or supernatural occurrences

- Tongues and interpretation

- Audible voice and so on.

Depending on one's level of consecration and God's plan, the Holy Spirit may use any vehicle to bring a word of knowledge and word of wisdom to someone. For me, I find that I receive inner pictures quite often. Sometimes these pictures come as parables or riddles and require interpretation. Other times they are clear messages needing no explanation.

The challenge with the gifts of the word of knowledge and word of wisdom, as with any other spiritual gift, is that sometimes people come for prayers and counseling expecting a word of knowledge or a word from God to them. This is not proper. We are not diviners. That is why we must teach people about the operation of these gifts. The gifts are not used as the minister wants. It is the Holy Spirit who determines when they should operate or not.

9. The Gift of Discernment of Spirits

₁₀ to another the working of miracles, to another prophecy, to another **discerning of spirits**, to another different kinds of tongues, to another the interpretation of tongues. – 1 Cor. 12:10

The gift of discernment of spirits is one gift every Christian needs to desire in these dangerous and perilous times. This gift enables someone to understand and distinguish between the operation of the human spirit, demonic spirits, and the Holy Spirit.

Not all prophecies are from God. Not all teachings are from God. Not all manifestations are from God. Many are actually from the devil, with a willful intent to deceive and harm. What happens in this gift is that the Holy Spirit will give you supernatural selectivity, judgment, and insight, involving prophecies, false teachers, and manifestations in the church. You will know, deep inside of you, without a shadow of a doubt, whether an operation is from God or not. Then you will be able to protect yourself, expose, and guide others properly.

For lack of discernment of spirits, many believers are surrendering daily to the operation of demons in the name of prophecies, miracles, and healings. Many ministers have brought false preachers into their churches that came and spiritually destroyed what they were building. We need discernment of spirits today, more than ever.

The gift of discernment is also very important in deliverance. With it, one can see through demonic manifestations and cast them out without struggles.

Declaration

I declare today that I have the wisdom to recognize God's gifts in my life. I have faith to let the gifts flow through me. And I have the opportunities to use God's gifts in my life for the glory of God, in Jesus name.

Amen.

Day 27: Types of Spiritual Gifts (4): Service Gifts

₆Having then gifts differing according to the grace that is given to us, let us use them: if prophecy, let us prophesy in proportion to our faith; ₇or ministry, let us use it in our ministering; he who teaches, in teaching; ₈he who exhorts, in exhortation; he who gives, with liberality; he who leads, with diligence; he who shows mercy, with cheerfulness. – Rom. 12: 6-8

Apart from the nine supernatural gifts so far discussed, the Apostle Paul wants us to understand that we can also receive natural abilities that function through the influence of the Holy Spirit. These natural gifts are also important and must be yielded to the Lord's service and used for His glory. Some of them are:

The Gift of Serving

The gift of serving others or assisting others is the ability to joyfully work together with others and help them complete the assignment God has given them. People with this gift usually prefer to work behind the scenes. They find joy in assisting others and helping alleviate the burdens and responsibilities of others. This gift is habitually accompanied by an attitude of humbleness and sacrifice.

If you have this gift, you will always desire to work in a supportive role than a leadership capacity. You will naturally enjoy helping others become more effective in their work. You will prefer to work behind the scenes. When someone is doing something poorly, your first instinct will be to help them rather than criticize.

The Gift of Teaching

The gift of teaching is the God-given ability to understand and communicate biblical truth in a clear and applicable manner so that there is understanding and use. People with the gift of teaching enjoy learning, researching, communicating, and illustrating truth of Scripture. They enjoy studying and learning new information, and find great joy in sharing it with others. The format of teaching varies from one-on-one discipleship to formal classes, informal Bible studies, large groups, and preaching.

The Gift of Administration

Administration includes the ability to organize people, resources, information, finances, etc. The mark of an administrator is the ability to accomplish things in an appropriate and orderly manner. The gift of administration is God's ability to give direction and make decisions that result in efficient operation and achievement of goals. People with the gift of administration have a keen eye for details, and proper organization, and problem-solving.

If you have this gift, you'll always feel frustrated when things are poorly organized, so much that you want to volunteer to fix them. You'll always have a burning desire to bring order out of disorder. You'll want to help with the organization of records, finances, projects, and tasks.

The Gift of Evangelism

People with the gift of evangelism passionately care about unsaved souls. They have a strong desire to see them meet Jesus. They feel compassion for the lost and seek to understand their questions and doubts so that they can provide a persuasive answer. People with this gift may prefer being with people instead of hanging out with Christians in the church. They enjoy sharing the Gospel and are happy when people give their lives to Christ.

The Gift of Encouragement

People with the gift of encouragement have an unusual sensitivity for and are attracted to those who are downcast or struggling. They are blessed with healing and gracious words and can encourage others in tough times. They are very patient with people, and as a result, people come to them for compassionate counsel.

If you're always passionate about speaking to people and helping them through their problems, and find it easy to connect with those who are suffering, then you may have this gift.

The Gift of Giving

The gift of giving is the ability to give money, and other forms of wealth joyfully, prudently, and generously to meet the needs of others, and help support ministries. People with this gift genuinely view their treasures, talents, and time as gifts from God and not their own. They are frequently moved to meet the physical needs of others. They enjoy giving of themselves and what they have. When they do not possess the resources to help, they earnestly pray for those needs to be met.

The Gift of Mercy

The gift of mercy is the capacity to feel and express unusual compassion and sympathy for those in difficult or crisis situations and provide them with the necessary help and support to see them through tough times. People with this gift have the ability to "walk in another's shoes" and feel the pain and burdens they carry. They desire to make a difference in the lives of hurting people without being judgmental.

The Gift of Hospitality

The gift of hospitality is the ability to welcome strangers and entertain guests, often in your home, with great joy and kindness so that they become friends. People with this gift often have an "open home" where others are welcome to visit. They enjoy watching people meet and have fun at parties and events they helped to plan and host, and always feel that something is missing in their lives when they cannot have guests in their homes. This gift is sometimes combined with the talent of design, cooking, and event planning.

Conclusion

6 God has given each of us the ability to do certain things well. So if God has given you the ability to prophesy, then prophesy whenever you can—as often as your faith is strong enough to receive a message from God.

7 If your gift is that of serving others, serve them well. If you are a teacher, do a good job of teaching. 8 If you are a preacher, see to it that your sermons are strong and helpful. If God has given you money, be generous in helping others with it. If God has given you administrative ability and put you in charge of the work of others, take the responsibility seriously. Those who offer comfort to the sorrowing should do so with Christian cheer. - Romans 12:5-8 (TLB)

Of course, we may not be able to cover all natural gifts that the Holy Spirit gifts to us and desires us to use for the improvement of the Body of Christ. But as we serve God from day to day and fellowship with other Christians, He will open doors and bring us face to face with needs and areas that our gifts will be useful. Learn to surrender to the Holy Spirit every day and genuinely desire to be of good use to the Lord. He will provide you with opportunities to function in His gift.

Declaration

Precious Holy Spirit, I surrender to You today and every day. I desire to be Your vessel of honor. When You open doors for me to use my gifts for Your service, please guide to yield to You. Use me to edify the Body of Christ and glorify the name of Jesus Christ always, in Jesus name.

Amen.

Day 28: How to Discover Your Spiritual Gifts

₄₄"The kingdom of heaven is like treasure hidden in a field. When a man found it, he hid it again, and then in his joy went and sold all he had and bought that field." - Matthew 13:44

Everyone has at least one spiritual gift, sometimes more. But all of God's gifts are like hidden treasures. You must seek to find them. You have to dig to discover.

So how do you dig to discover your spiritual gifts?

Pray For Guidance

Jesus said, *Ask, and it will be given to you; seek and you will find; knock, and it will be opened to you. For everyone who asks receives, and he who seeks finds, and to him who knocks it will be opened* (Matthew 7:7-8). If you're wondering what your spiritual gifts are, ask God. Connect with Him in a heartfelt, sincere prayer. He is the Giver of the gifts, and it is His good pleasure to see you bear fruits for the Kingdom. He will arrange circumstances and situations that will reveal your spiritual gifts without a shadow of a doubt.

Look Inward

This means to check your personality. What are your strengths, passions, and hobbies? Sometimes your spiritual gifts may be connected to your personality. *"For it is God who works in you both to will and to do for His good pleasure"* (Philippians 2:13).

Look Outward

What are your experiences? God may also use your experiences to unravel your spiritual gifts. If He gives you a gift of mercy and hospitality, He may let you go through the misery of homelessness in order to feel what it means to be homeless and hopeless. His assignment to you to encourage single parents or those who suffer all kinds of abuse can be unveiled through the abuse you went through.

Don't let your messy situation mess you up; it can be a medium through which God wants to unravel your message of hope to others.

Feedback

Apart from your personal experiences, people can also confirm the gifts of God in your life. People who know you well and want to be sincere with you can tell you the area you are very good at and most times they are correct.

Study Spiritual Gifts

While reading God's word, and studying the subject of spiritual gifts through books, tapes, and videos, you'll most likely find the answer your heart seeks. I discerned my spiritual gifts during such a study. Most times, when you set out to find answers about a particular subject, the Holy Spirit arranges the answers for you on the way. Remember, the Word says, "seek and you shall find." Through targeted study and research, you can discover what your spiritual gifts are.

Start From Somewhere

Get busy for God. Don't wait until you hear a voice. Sometimes God guides you into your gifts as you begin to do something for Him. In your kingdom busy-ness, you will be guided into what you should be doing.

Declaration

Today,

I declare that as I ask, I shall receive; as I seek, I shall find; and as I knock, the door shall be opened for me. I will find out what my spiritual gifts are and I shall bring glory to God in my life, in Jesus name.

Amen.

Day 29: Facts About Spiritual Gifts

Spiritual gifts are a means to an end, not the end. While they are very important in our lives, God's Kingdom is the end goal. So here are some important facts to keep in mind while chasing spiritual gifts:

Everyone in the Body of Christ Has a Spiritual Gift

All these things [the gifts, the achievements, the abilities, the empowering] are brought about by one and the same Holy Spirit, distributing to each one individually just as He chooses. - 1 Corinthians 12:11 (AMP)

You have at least one spiritual gift, if not more. Every Christian has some spiritual gifts deposited in them by the Holy Spirit. You don't need to feel it to know that you have spiritual gifts. You just need to prayerfully discern your gifts.

God Gives to Everyone As He Wills

But now [as things really are], God has placed and arranged the parts in the body, each one of them, just as He willed and saw fit [with the best balance of function]. - 1 Corinthians 12:18 (AMP)

God is our Maker. He understands us more than everyone else and knows the gifts that are best fitted for our persons and purposes. We may desire certain gifts, but we do not decide what gifts we must choose and use. We only need to surrender to His work in our lives.

We Are Not Gifted Equally

"For the kingdom of heaven is like a man traveling to a far country, who called his own servants and delivered his goods to them. 15 And to one he gave five talents, to another two, and to another one, to each according to his own ability; and immediately he went on a journey. - Matthew 25:14-15

The good man divided His talents among his servants according to their several abilities. The talents they received were proportional to their strengths and capacities. None of them was under-gifted, and none was over-gifted.

The Holy Spirit gifts us according to His assignment for our lives. Some will have more gifts than others.

But there is no need for envy and spitefulness. We are only to yield to the Holy Spirit at all times, and He will use us to glorify God always.

You Can Have More if You Are Faithful

You are gifted for a purpose. God is not waiting until the last day for you to give an account of your gifts. He is checking up on you every day to see what's happening with the gifts He has put in you. If you are faithfully learning and trying to use the gifts for His glory, He'll be pleased to continue adding more gifts into your life.

You Can Lose Divine Opportunities

God does not withdraw His gifts and callings from our lives (Romans 11:29). He does not change His mind on what He has made us to be. But if we persistently live in sin, we may lose His opportunities to bear fruits and excel in life. And we will also lose his heavenly kingdom.

Spiritual Gifts Does Not Guarantee Heaven

21 "Not everyone who says to Me, 'Lord, Lord,' shall enter the kingdom of heaven, but he who does the will of My Father in heaven. 22 Many will say to Me in that day, 'Lord, Lord, have we not prophesied in Your name, cast out demons in Your name, and done many wonders in Your name?' *₂₃ And then I will declare to them, 'I never knew you; depart from Me, you who practice lawlessness!'* - Matthew 7:21-23

> **You can cast out demons, heal the sick, perform miracles, prophesy, and do many wonders in God's name, but still end up in hell fire.**

The people Jesus talked about here were not necessarily false teachers and false miracle workers. They did what they did in the name of Christ, but were surprised that they were rejected on the last day. If they were intentional false prophets and teachers, they wouldn't be surprised. They must have operated in the gifts of the Holy Spirit but lacked the fruits of the Spirit.

The gifts of the Spirit empower your service to God, while the fruit of the Spirit develops your character.

Gifts are what we possess, but the fruit of the Spirit is what we become. Spiritual gifts will one day cease, while spiritual fruits are permanent.

> But the fruit of the Spirit is love, joy, peace, longsuffering, kindness, goodness, faithfulness, gentleness, self-control. Against such, there is no law - Galatians 5:22-23.

While seeking to develop your spiritual gifts, you need to make room for the fruits of the Holy Spirit. Spiritual gifts will make you useful to the Body of Christ, but Godly character will make you long-lasting and get you to heaven.

If you're an adulterer and an unreliable person, but who can prophesy and do miracles, it's only a matter of time before you get yourself shipwrecked. But you have the opportunity to repent and recommit yourself to God today.

Many Christians speak in tongues, prophesy and pray all manner of fire prayers, but have deep character flaws. They defraud, lie, hurt others without remorse, and do whatever they want without minding the consequences. They are gifted but their lives are not reflecting the fruits of the Spirit. These Christians are not true ambassadors of Christ.

The gifts without the fruits lead to disaster. Spiritual gifts do not guarantee us a place in God's Kingdom. It is the fruit of the Holy Spirit that leads us to heaven.

Declaration

Precious Holy Spirit,

I desire to manifest Your gifts in my life. I desire to be useful to the Body of Christ. But I also desire much more to be a true ambassador whose life reflects the fruits of the Holy Spirit, in Jesus name.

Amen.

Day 30: Prayers for Spiritual Gifts

₄There are diversities of gifts, but the same Spirit. ₅There are differences of ministries, but the same Lord. ₆And there are diversities of activities, but it is the same God who works all in all. ₇But the manifestation of the Spirit is given to each one for the profit of all. - 1 Corinthians 12:4-7

Let's dedicate today and pray for the gifts of the Holy Spirit.

Meditation Scriptures

1 Corinthians 12: 1-31 -Now concerning spiritual gifts, brethren, I do not want you to be ignorant ... (Read all chapter).

1 Peter 4:10 - As each one has received a gift, minister it to one another, as good stewards of the manifold grace of God.

Romans 12:6-8 - ₆ Having then gifts differing according to the grace that is given to us, let us use them: if prophecy, let us prophesy in proportion to our faith; ₇ or ministry, let us use it in our ministering; he who teaches, in teaching; ₈ he who exhorts, in exhortation; he who gives, with liberality; he who leads, with diligence; he who shows mercy, with cheerfulness.

1 Timothy 4:14-15 - ₁₄ Do not neglect the gift that is in you, which was given to you by prophecy with the laying on of the hands of the eldership. ₁₅ Meditate on these things; give yourself entirely to them, that your progress may be evident to all.

1 Corinthians 14:1-40 - Follow after charity, and desire spiritual gifts, but rather that ye may prophesy... (Read all)

Ephesians 4:11 - And he gave some, apostles; and some, prophets; and some, evangelists; and some, pastors and teachers.

Prayers

Dear Holy Spirit, You are the One here on earth today testifying of Christ and bearing witness of His death and resurrection.

I surrender myself to You today, knowing fully well that One united with You is united with God the Father and our Savior, Jesus Christ.

Holy Spirit, I desire Your gifts, and I come asking You to brood upon me and manifest Your presence in my life and fill me with the Glory of Heaven, in Jesus name.

Holy Spirit, I give You my heart and I offer my passionate thanksgiving for all the grace which You never cease to impart on me. Manifest in me the gifts which You have bestowed on me for my spiritual instruction, and benefiting of Your people, in Jesus name.

Dear Holy Spirit, Your Word reveals different gifts that come from You, given to us, individually, to serve the Body of Christ. These gifts, according to 1 Corinthians 12:7-11 include:

- The gift of the word of wisdom
- The gift of the word of knowledge
- The gift of faith
- The gift of healing
- The gift of performing miracles
- The gift of prophecy
- The gift of discernment of spirits
- The gift of speaking in different tongues,
- The gift of interpreting different tongues.
- The gift of giving
- The gift of hospitality
- The gift of administration
- The gift of evangelism
- The gift of teaching
- The gift of mercy
- The gift of help

Holy Spirit, if You ask me, I would say that I need all of these gifts. However, I know there is a gift or several gifts You have already imparted in me. Cause me to recognize this gift or these gifts and let them manifest in my life, in such a way I would be so convinced of Your Work in my life, in Jesus name.

Holy Spirit, please make me humble even as I serve Your people with the gifts You have bestowed on me, which begins to flow and manifest in undeniable ways in my life henceforth, in Jesus name.

Thank You, Holy Spirit, for answered prayers.

Day 31: Fellowship with the Holy Spirit

The grace of the Lord Jesus Christ, and the love of God, and the communion of the Holy Spirit be with you all. Amen. - 2 Corinthians 13:14

In the Old Testament, the Holy Spirit was coming and going, anointing individuals for specific assignments. He was not permanent on earth. But on the day of Pentecost, He came on the Apostles. He is here today and will remain here until after the rapture of the saints.

The Holy Spirit is here as our Mentor - to teach, guide, and instruct us. Because He is God, He is All-knowing. He knows everything about everything.

The Holy Spirit can also be a reliable friend. He can keep us company in isolation. He is not only residing in us. He is also walking side by side with us.

The Apostle Paul, in today's reading, calls us to maintain fellowship with the Holy Spirit. Fellowship involves friendly association, communication, and partnership.

Fellowship with the Holy Spirit is the only way to learn more about God and make room for His gifts and fruits in our lives.

The Holy Spirit Is a Wise Counselor

The Holy Spirit will counsel you on how to live a productive life, how to become a successful wife, mother, and minister. He will counsel you on how to succeed in business, how to succeed with your spouse, and with others. He will counsel you on how to maintain a good relationship with your boss or subordinates. The Holy Spirit can counsel you on just about every aspect of life.

The Holy Spirit Will Defend You

The Holy Spirit is a gentle dove, but He is also a mighty rushing wind and the Spirit of judgment. He will help you overcome the wicked traps of men and defend you from sudden attacks of evil ones.

The Holy Spirit Will Help You

The Holy Spirit is a wonderful Helper. He will help you in your times of need. And believe me, you will have many times of need in your life. He will help you in prayers. He will help you in your assignment. He will help you live peacefully with others.

The Holy Spirit Will Give You Ideas

The Holy Spirit will give you ideas that will make you succeed in life. He will inspire you on the kind of work you should do to stand out in your world. He will inspire you to be outstanding in your field of endeavor. If you are a singer, writer, preacher, teacher, businessman, civil servant, or student, whatever you are, the Holy Spirit will inspire you on how to become the best

The key is to learn to fellowship with the Holy Spirit.

How?

Be Conscious of His Presence

Whether you feel He is with you or not does not make any difference; He is always there. Learn to acknowledge Him from time to time. He is a sensitive person. If you recognize Him and give Him attention, He will guide you in the most amazing ways.

Commune With Him

The Holy Spirit is not a force; He is a person. He wants you to talk to Him about everything. As a friend you can trust, He will not only help you, He will also fight for you.

Learn the Power of Praise and Worship

As a third Person in the Godhead, the Holy Spirit inhabits praise and worship. When you are praising and worshipping God, you are creating a comfortable atmosphere for His manifestation.

Study the Word

The Word is the food of the Holy Spirit. When you are reading and meditating on the Word, you are giving the Holy Spirit room in your life, empowering your spirit to connect with Him.

Pray Often in the Holy Ghost (Jude 20)

20 But you, beloved, building yourselves up on your most holy faith, praying in the Holy Spirit, 21 keep yourselves in the love of God, looking for the mercy of our Lord Jesus Christ unto eternal life. – Jude 1:20-21

Praying in the Holy Spirit triggers the presence of the Holy Spirit. As much as He empowers you, pray in the Holy Spirit often.

Declaration

Holy Spirit, I welcome You into my life today and every day. I surrender to Your leading and work in my life. I acknowledge Your presence, which is always with me. As I learn to commune and fellowship with You onwards, I know You will bring out the best in me, and help me fulfill God's plan for my life, every day, in Jesus name.

Amen.

God

Bless

You!

Get in Touch

We love testimonies.

We love to hear what God is doing around the world as people draw close to Him in prayer. If this book has blessed...

Please share your story with us.

Also, please consider giving this book a review on Amazon and checking out our other titles at:

www. amazon.com/author/danielokpara.

Kindly check out our website at www.BetterLifeWorld.org, and send us your prayer request. As we join faith with you, God's power will be made manifest in your life.

Other Books by the Same Author

1. Prayer Retreat: 21 Days Devotional With Over 500 Prayers & Declarations to Destroy Stubborn Demonic Problems.

2. HEALING PRAYERS & CONFESSIONS

3. 200 Violent Prayers for Deliverance, Healing, and Financial Breakthrough.

4. Hearing God's Voice in Painful Moments

5. Healing Prayers: Prophetic Prayers that Brings Healing

6. Healing WORDS: Daily Confessions & Declarations to Activate Your Healing.

7. Prayers That Break Curses and Spells and Release Favors and Breakthroughs.

8. 120 Powerful Night Prayers That Will Change Your Life Forever.

9. How to Pray for Your Children Everyday

10. How to Pray for Your Family

11. Daily Prayer Guide

12. Make Him Respect You: 31 Very Important Relationship Intelligence for Women to Make their Men Respect them.

13. How to Cast Out Demons from Your Home, Office & Property

14. Praying Through the Book of Psalms

15. The Students' Prayer Book

16. How to Pray and Receive Financial Miracle

17. Powerful Prayers to Destroy Witchcraft Attacks.

18. Deliverance from Marine Spirits

19. Deliverance From Python Spirit

20. Anger Management God's Way

21. How God Speaks to You

22. Deliverance of the Mind

23. 20 Commonly Asked Questions About Demons

24. Praying the Promises of God

25. When God Is Silent! What to Do When Prayer Seems Unanswered or Delayed

26. I SHALL NOT DIE: Prayers to Overcome the Spirit and Fear of Death.

27. Praise Warfare

28. Prayers to Find a Godly Spouse

29. How to Exercise Authority Over Sickness

30. Under His Shadow: Praying the Promises of God for Protection (Book 2).

About the Author

Daniel Chika Okpara is an influential voice in contemporary Christian ministry. His mandate is to make lives better through the teaching and preaching of God's Word with signs and wonders. He is the resident pastor of Shining Light Christian Centre, a fast-growing church in the city of Lagos.

He is also the president and CEO of Better Life World Outreach Center, a non-denominational ministry dedicated to global evangelism, prayer revival and empowering of God's people with the WORD to make their lives better. Through his Breakthrough Prayers Foundation (www.breakthroughprayers.org), an online portal leading people all over the world to encounter God and change their lives through prayer, thousands of people encounter God through prayer, and hundreds of testimonies are received from all around the world.

As a foremost Christian teacher and author, his books are in high demand in prayer groups, Bible studies, and for personal devotions. He has authored over 50 life-transforming books and manuals on business, prayer, relationship and victorious living, many of which have become international best-sellers.

He is a Computer Engineer by training and holds a Master's Degree in Christian Education from Continental Christian University. He is married to Doris Okpara, his best friend, and the most significant support in his life. They are blessed with lovely children.

WEBSITE: www.betterlifeworld.org

NOTES

Made in the USA
Middletown, DE
06 November 2023

42077944R00099